THE LITTLE ENGINEER COLORING BOOK

HOW TO BUILD A HOUSE

SETH MCKAY

The Little Engineer Coloring Book: How to Build a House by Seth McKay
www.TheLittleEngineerBooks.com

Copyright © 2018 by Seth McKay

Creative Ideas Publishing titles may be purchased in bulk for educational, business, fund-raising, or sales promotional use. For information, please email permissions@TheLittleEngineerBooks.com.

ISBN-13: 978-1-722070-91-5

Published by: Creative Ideas Publishing

Table of Contents

Introduction *(for parents)*

Thank you so much for your interest in this book. In these books, your child will be introduced to new, interesting topics and begin to understand how things work.

I've always wanted my children to understand how things work, and in general, understand that objects are not magical boxes that work for some unknown reason. I want them to understand that objects are quite simple when broken down into a few key components. Without any direction, it is possible for a child to get the wrong understanding of objects that we consider to be simple.

For example, we understand that a printer has a roller that moves the paper and a little ink jet that sprays the paper with ink as it rolls by to make images. However, it would be very easy for our children to see the same printer and conclude that this magic box shoots out paper, and this is where paper comes from.

I chose to make this book a coloring book because I wanted to ensure that the book was also fun! I don't want this book to be too serious, boring or overwhelming. Coloring helps keep the book fun while incorporating new and challenging topics.

Book Objective:

The objective of this book is not to make your child an engineer (I hope your child chooses whatever career path suits him or her best), and the objective is not for your child to know exactly how everything works and memorize each step of building a house.

The objective is simply to begin to introduce your child to new, interesting concepts that might catch his or her attention and help your child understand that seemingly complex things are just a few simple items put together.

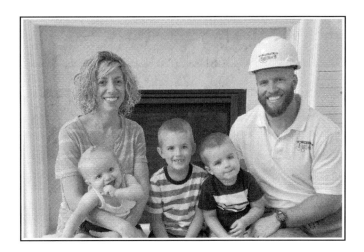

Introduction *(for the Little Engineers)*

Hello Little Engineer!

My name is Seth, and I'm the Chief Engineer of this book. I'm so happy you have this book so we can learn how to build a house together. Of course, we are going to have fun too!

We will start with an empty field, then build a nice big house, discover where the water comes from that ends up in our bath tub, and even learn how appliances work.

Enjoy coloring, ask your parents lots of questions, and most of all, have fun!

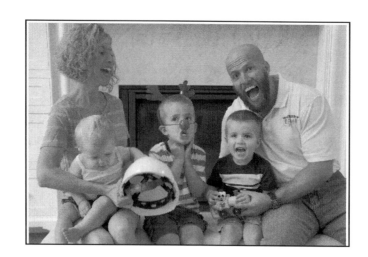

Tips on Using this Book

- **Read the book as a story to your child** – Before coloring the book, read it one time as a full story to help your child get a sense of the "big picture" before they focus on a single page to color.

- **Add your own explanations** – You know your child best so take the wording on a page and expand on it to help your child understand.

- **Relate the pages to your surroundings** – Not all houses are the same, so a picture might not match your house so be sure to point out how this house is different from your house. For example, you may have a metal roof, but this book mentions shingles.

- **Take a field trip** – Stop by a half built neighborhood or point out objects like water towers. This will allow your child to understand that these are real objects that we use everyday.

LET'S GET STARTED!

SURVEY THE LAND

SURVEY LEVEL

THE LAND SURVEYOR HELPS FIND THE PERFECT SPOT FOR A NEW HOUSE TO BE BUILT.

THE SURVEY LEVEL TOOL HELPS THE LAND SURVEYOR MEASURE HOW TALL A HILL IS.

Back of coloring page left blank intentionally to allow for marker use.

PREPARE THE LAND

BULLDOZER

A BIG BULLDOZER
SMOOTHES AND FLATTENS THE DIRT.

Back of coloring page left blank intentionally to allow for marker use.

AN ARCHITECT DRAWS THE HOUSE

COMPUTER

DRAWING TABLE

BLUEPRINT

AN ARCHITECT DESIGNS THE HOUSE AND MAKES BLUEPRINTS TO GIVE TO THE BUILDERS.

BLUEPRINTS ARE THE INSTRUCTIONS THAT SHOW THE BUILDERS HOW TO BUILD THE HOUSE.

Back of coloring page left blank intentionally to allow for marker use.

CONCRETE TRUCKS HELP MAKE THE FOUNDATION

CONCRETE TRUCK

BUILDERS USE THE BLUEPRINTS AND MAKE THE FOUNDATION
OF THE HOUSE TO MATCH THE BLUEPRINT DRAWINGS.
THE FOUNDATION IS MADE OF CONCRETE.
A BIG CONCRETE TRUCK COMES TO THE HOUSE
AND POURS CONCRETE TO MAKE THE FOUNDATION.

Back of coloring page left blank intentionally to allow for marker use.

A TRUCK DELIVERS BUILDING SUPPLIES

CRANE

BUILDING SUPPLIES

A TRUCK DELIVERS BUILDING SUPPLIES TO THE HOUSE.
BIG PIECES OF WOOD ARE DELIVERED
AND MOVED OFF THE TRUCK
USING A CRANE OR FORKLIFT.

Back of coloring page left blank intentionally to allow for marker use.

WALLS ARE BUILT

STUD

THE BUILDERS USE PIECES OF WOOD TO BUILD WALLS
ON THE FOUNDATION.
THE TALL PIECES OF WOOD IN THE WALL ARE CALLED STUDS.
THERE IS A TOOL CALLED A "STUD FINDER" THAT CAN
HELP YOU FIND STUDS INSIDE YOUR OWN WALLS.

Back of coloring page left blank intentionally to allow for marker use.

HOW TO HOLD WALLS TOGETHER

WOOD

SCREW

DRILL

WOOD

NAIL

HAMMER

THE BUILDERS USE SCREWS OR NAILS
TO HOLD THE WALLS TOGETHER.

Back of coloring page left blank intentionally to allow for marker use.

ADD WINDOWS

BUILDERS LEAVE BIG SQUARE OR RECTANGULAR
HOLES IN THE WALLS;
LATER THEY INSTALL WINDOWS IN THESE HOLES.
WINDOWS ARE MADE AT A FACTORY, AND DELIVERED
TO THE HOUSE READY TO FIT INTO THE WALLS.

Back of coloring page left blank intentionally to allow for marker use.

ADD THE ROOF

CRANE

ROOF

LADDER

A CRANE LOWERS THE ROOF ONTO THE HOUSE.
A WATERPROOF SHEET IS THEN PUT
ON TOP OF THE ROOF,
AND SHINGLES ADDED ON TOP OF THAT.

Back of coloring page left blank intentionally to allow for marker use.

ADD WATER PIPES

A PLUMBER ADDS PIPES INSIDE THE WALLS FOR WATER.
THE PIPES MOVE WATER TO DIFFERENT ROOMS
INSIDE THE HOUSE. BATHROOMS, KITCHENS
AND LAUNDRY ROOMS ALL NEED WATER PIPES.

Back of coloring page left blank intentionally to allow for marker use.

ADD WIRES FOR ELECTRICITY

LIGHTS

WIRE

SWITCH

POWER OUTLET

AN ELECTRICIAN ADDS WIRES IN THE WALLS.
THESE WIRES CARRY ELECTRICITY TO THE LIGHTS,
OUTLETS, FANS, REFRIGERATOR AND ANYTHING ELSE
THAT NEEDS ELECTRICITY.

Back of coloring page left blank intentionally to allow for marker use.

COVER THE WALLS, PIPES, AND WIRES

SHEETROCK

SHEETROCK MUD

THE INSIDE OF THE WALLS ARE COVERED BY
BIG FLAT SHEETS CALLED SHEETROCK.
SCREWS HOLD THE SHEETROCK UP ONTO THE WALLS;
THE SCREWS ARE THEN HIDDEN BY COVERING THEM
WITH 'SHEETROCK MUD' AND PAINT.

Back of coloring page left blank intentionally to allow for marker use.

ADD AN AIR CONDITIONER

AIR CONDITIONERS HELP KEEP THE AIR INSIDE THE HOUSE
FROM GETTING TOO HOT OR COLD. ON A HOT DAY,
THE AIR CONDITIONER PULLS HEAT OUT OF THE AIR
AND SENDS IT OUT OF THE HOUSE;
THIS MAKES THE AIR INSIDE THE HOUSE NICE AND COOL.

Back of coloring page left blank intentionally to allow for marker use.

NOW THE HOUSE IS READY!

LET'S CONNECT THE HOUSE TO THE TOWN'S ELECTRICAL POWER LINES AND WATER PIPES.

ELECTRICAL WIRES

WATER PIPE

THE POWER COMPANY CONNECTS THE HOUSE'S
ELECTRICAL WIRES TO TALL POWER LINES.
SOMETIMES THESE POWER LINES ARE UNDERGROUND.
THE WATER COMPANY CONNECTS THE HOUSE'S
WATER PIPES TO A BIG WATER PIPE THAT IS BY THE ROAD.

Back of coloring page left blank intentionally to allow for marker use.

WHERE DOES THE ELECTRICITY COME FROM?

POWER LINES

HOUSE

POWER PLANT

HUGE FACTORIES CALLED "POWER PLANTS"
MAKE ELECTRICITY FOR THOUSANDS OF HOUSES!
THE NEXT FOUR PAGES WILL SHOW
HOW THE POWER PLANTS MAKE ELECTRICITY.

Back of coloring page left blank intentionally to allow for marker use.

FUEL POWER PLANT

GAS TURBINE AND BOILER POWER PLANT

FUEL

FUEL

GENERATOR

BURNER

THE POWER PLANT BURNS FUEL TO SPIN A GENERATOR. THE
SPINNING GENERATOR MAKES ELECTRICITY.
SOMETIMES WATER IS HEATED UP TO MAKE STEAM, AND
THAT STEAM IS STRONG ENOUGH TO SPIN THE GENERATOR.

Back of coloring page left blank intentionally to allow for marker use.

MOViNG WATER POWER PLANT

HYDROELECTRIC POWER PLANT

DAM

DAM

WATER

GENERATOR

A DAM IS A BIG WALL THAT STOPS WATER AND MAKES A LAKE. THE BIG WALL HAS A PIPE INSIDE TO LET THE WATER FALL DOWN THE PIPE AND THE FALLING WATER SPINS A GENERATOR TO MAKE ELECTRICITY.

Back of coloring page left blank intentionally to allow for marker use.

SUN POWER PLANT

SOLAR PANEL POWER PLANT

INVERTER

ENERGY FROM THE SUN

SOLAR PANEL

ELECTRICITY GOES TO HOUSE

SUN POWER PLANTS CAN HAVE THOUSANDS
OF SOLAR PANELS.
SOLAR PANELS TAKE THE BRIGHT ENERGY
FROM THE SUN AND CHANGE IT INTO ELECTRICITY.

Back of coloring page left blank intentionally to allow for marker use.

WIND POWER PLANT

WIND TURBINE POWER PLANT

A WIND TURBINE CAN BE TALLER
THAN A 30 STORY BUILDING!
WIND PUSHES THE BLADES AROUND WHICH SPINS
THE GENERATOR TO MAKE ELECTRICITY.

Back of coloring page left blank intentionally to allow for marker use.

MAKING POWER AT YOUR HOUSE

WIND TURBINE

SOLAR PANELS

**ELECTRICITY CAN BE MADE AT YOUR HOUSE TOO!
SOLAR PANELS AND WIND TURBINES
CAN BE INSTALLED AT YOUR HOUSE;
IT IS LIKE HAVING YOUR OWN TINY POWER PLANT!**

Back of coloring page left blank intentionally to allow for marker use.

WHERE DOES WATER COME FROM?

WATER TOWER

WATER GOING TO HOUSE

WATER TREATMENT PLANT

THE HOUSE'S WATER PIPES ARE CONNECTED TO TALL WATER TOWERS. THE WATER FALLS DOWN THE TOWER AND INTO THE HOUSE WHEN THE WATER IS TURNED ON; THIS IS WHY WATER COMES OUT OF THE FAUCET OR SHOWER QUICKLY.

Back of coloring page left blank intentionally to allow for marker use.

HOW THE WATER IS CLEANED

WATER TOWER

LAKE

WATER TREATMENT PLANT

1ST FILTER TO CATCH BIG ITEMS LIKE STICKS

WATER MOVES SLOWLY THROUGH BIG POOLS SO DIRT FALLS TO THE BOTTOM

DIRT

BIG FILTERS CLEAN THE WATER EVEN MORE

UV LIGHT CLEANS THE GERMS

WATER PUMP

THE WATER TREATMENT PLANT CLEANS ALL THE WATER
TO MAKE IT SAFE TO DRINK.
A WATER PUMP THEN PUMPS ALL THE WATER
UP INOT THE WATER TOWER.

Back of coloring page left blank intentionally to allow for marker use.

WELL WATER

WATER TANK

PUMP HOUSE

FILTER

WELL

WATER PUMP

SOME HOUSES ARE NOT CONNECTED TO A WATER TOWER
SO THESE HOUSES HAVE A DEEP HOLE CALLED A WELL.
A PUMP PUSHES WATER OUT OF THE WELL,
THROUGH A FILTER, AND THEN THE WATER IS
PUT INTO A WATER TANK.

Back of coloring page left blank intentionally to allow for marker use.

HOUSE COMPLETE!

THE HOUSE IS COMPLETE, AND WE KNOW HOW THE WATER
AND ELECTRICITY GET TO THE HOUSE.
NOW LET'S ADD A FEW MACHINES TO MAKE LIFE EASIER.
THESE MACHINES ARE CALLED APPLIANCES.

Back of coloring page left blank intentionally to allow for marker use.

HOT WATER HEATER

HOT WATER

COLD WATER

TEMPERATURE SENSOR

HEATER

DRAIN VALVE

THE HOT WATER HEATER MAKES THE WATER HOT SO THAT A BATH OR SHOWER CAN HAVE HOT WATER.
WITHOUT IT, ALL THE WATER IN YOUR HOUSE WOULD BE COLD LIKE THE WATER THAT COMES OUT OF THE HOSE OUTSIDE. THE HOT WATER HEATER IS A BIG TANK OF WATER AND A HEATER MAKES ALL THE WATER IN THE TANK HOT. THERE ARE ALSO HOT WATER HEATERS THAT DON'T HAVE A TANK OF WATER.

Back of coloring page left blank intentionally to allow for marker use.

REFRIGERATOR

HOT COILS

COMPRESSOR MOTOR

THE REFRIGERATOR KEEPS FOOD AND DRINKS COLD.
A REFRIGERATOR WORKS JUST LIKE
THE AIR CONDITIONING SYSTEM FOR THE HOUSE.
THE REFRIGERATOR PUMPS A SPECIAL FLUID,
CALLED REFRIGERANT, THROUGH THE PIPES.
THE PIPES MOVE HEAT FROM INSIDE THE REFRIGERATOR
TO THE HOT METAL PIPES BEHIND THE REFRIGERATOR.

Back of coloring page left blank intentionally to allow for marker use.

OVEN

OVEN TEMPERATURE CONTROL

COOKTOP HEATER

TEMPERATURE SENSOR

HEATER

THE OVEN IS THE MAIN APPLIANCE FOR COOKING FOOD,
AND IT EVEN BAKES COOKIES!
THE OVEN USES A POWERFUL HEATER TO MAKE THE INSIDE
OF THE OVEN VERY HOT. THE INSIDE OF AN OVEN
CAN REACH 500 DEGREES FAHRENHEIT.
THE COOK TOP HEATERS ARE USED FOR COOKING
WITH POTS - LIKE COOKING SPAGHETTI.

Back of coloring page left blank intentionally to allow for marker use.

DISHWASHER

HEATER

WATER SPRAY

WATER DRAIN PIPE

WATER PIPE

THE DISHWASHER QUICKLY CLEANS ALL THE DISHES.
THE DISHWASHER USES FAST MOVING WATER
AND SOAP TO CLEAN THE DISHES.
THE HEATER THEN TURNS ON AND DRIES
ALL THE WET DISHES.

Back of coloring page left blank intentionally to allow for marker use.

BLENDER

A BLENDER MIXES FOOD TOGETHER; IT CAN DO THINGS LIKE
MAKE A FRUIT SMOOTHIE OR MIX TOGETHER SALSA.
A BLENDER CHOPS UP FOOD WITH A BLADE THAT SPINS
REALLY FAST! THE BLADE IS CONNECTED TO A MOTOR,
AND THE MOTOR IS WHAT MAKES THE BLADE SPIN.
A CIRCLE KNOB CALLED A SPEED SELECTOR
TELLS THE MOTOR HOW FAST TO SPIN.

Back of coloring page left blank intentionally to allow for marker use.

WASHING MACHINE

WATER SUPPLY HOSES

TIME CONTROL

DRAIN HOSE

TUB

AGITATOR

MOTOR

THE WASHING MACHINE CLEANS ALL THE DIRTY CLOTHES.
THE WASHING MACHINE USES WATER AND SOAP
AND THEN SPINS AROUND TO HELP GET
ALL OF THE DIRT OFF OF THE CLOTHES.
WHEN FINISHED, THE CLOTHES ARE STILL WET
SO THEY HAVE TO BE PUT IN A DRYER.

Back of coloring page left blank intentionally to allow for marker use.

DRYER

THE DRYER HEATS UP CLOTHES UNTIL
THEY ARE DRY AND READY TO WEAR.
THE DRUM SPINS TO TUMBLE THE CLOTHES
WHILE THE HEATER MAKES ALL THE CLOTHES HOT.

Back of coloring page left blank intentionally to allow for marker use.

OUTDOOR GRILL

THERMOMETER

FIRE

BURNER

FUEL

A GRILL IS USUALLY OUTSIDE, AND IS USED TO COOK FOOD.
THE BURNER USES FUEL TO MAKE A TINY FIRE IN THE GRILL.
THE FIRE MAKES THE GRILL HOT FOR COOKING.

Back of coloring page left blank intentionally to allow for marker use.

Congratulations! Training Complete

You are now certified and have successfully completed your House Building Training!

Go to: thelittleengineerbooks.com/tle-house-certificate or scan the QR code, and enter your email to get a ready-to-print certificate

Certificate of Completion

This Certifies That

_____

Has Successfully Trained & Completed the

HOW TO BUILD A HOUSE TRAINING

And is Awarded This Certificate by

THE LITTLE ENGINEER

Parent/Guardian Signature: _____ Date: _____

SPECIAL PREVIEW

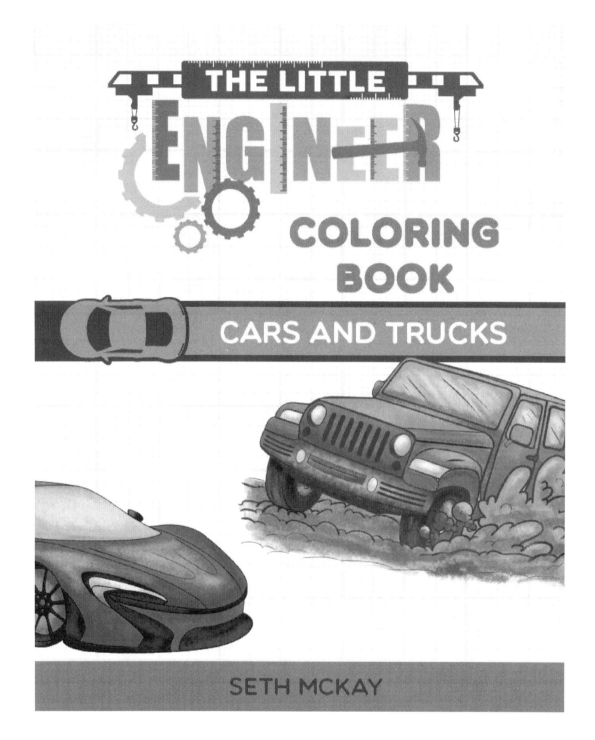

THE LITTLE **ENGINEER** COLORING BOOK

CARS AND TRUCKS

SETH MCKAY

Check out this short preview of another fun coloring book!

ENGINE ACCESSORIES

THE ENGINE ACCESSORIES ARE POWERED BY A BELT ON THE ENGINE. THE BELT SPINS THE WHEELS ON THE ACCESSORIES WHEN THE ENGINE IS ON.

• THE ALTERNATOR IS THE BATTERY CHARGER FOR THE CAR. IT IS A SMALL POWER GENERATOR THAT MAKES SURE YOUR CAR HAS PLENTY OF ELECTRICITY FOR LIGHTS, SPARK PLUGS, THE RADIO AND MORE.

• THE AC COMPRESSOR HELPS THE AC SYSTEM WORK SO THE AIR IS NICE AND COLD INSIDE THE CAR.

• THE POWER STEERING PUMP MAKES IT EASIER TO TURN THE STEERING WHEEL.

RADIATOR

HOT
COOLANT

RADIATOR

COLD
COOLANT

ENGINES GET VERY HOT.

- A RADIATOR HELPS KEEP THE ENGINE FROM GETTING TOO HOT.
- A WATER PUMP MOVES A SPECIAL LIQUID CALLED COOLANT THROUGH THE ENGINE AND THEN THROUGH A RADIATOR.

2 DiFFERENTiALS

REAR DiFFERENTiAL

FRONT DiFFERENTiAL

ON TRUCKS, YOU CAN SOMETIMES SEE 2 DIFFERENTIALS.
THIS MEANS THE TRUCK HAS 4-WHEEL DRIVE.
SOME CARS HAVE 4-WHEEL DRIVE, BUT IT IS HARD
TO SEE THE DIFFERENTIAL BECAUSE THE CAR IS
CLOSE TO THE GROUND.

The Little Engineer Coloring Book: Cars and Trucks

TWiN TURBOCHARGERS

TURBOCHARGERS

THIS CAR HAS 2 TURBOCHARGERS!

MOST TURBOCHARGERS ARE UNDER THE HOOD AND HARD TO SEE, BUT SOME CARS HAVE THEM STICKING OUT OF THE HOOD WHICH IS REALLY COOL!

FRONT, MID AND REAR ENGINE

FRONT

MID

REAR

THERE ARE FRONT, MID AND REAR ENGINE CARS.

- FRONT ENGINE CARS HAVE THE ENGINE BETWEEN THE FRONT WHEELS AND THE FRONT OF THE CAR.
- MID ENGINE CARS HAVE THE ENGINE BETWEEN THE FRONT AND REAR WHEELS.
- REAR ENGINE CARS HAVE THE ENGINE BETWEEN THE BACK WHEELS AND BACK OF THE CAR.

We hope you enjoyed the book!
Contact us anytime at CreativeIdeasPublishing.com

We are a US based publisher that consist of parents and teachers. We try our best to make products that our kids will love and we hope your kids love them too!

Ask your bookstore for more great titles from
Creative Ideas Publishing!

Made in the USA
Las Vegas, NV
14 November 2023

80855612R00046